Uncommon Vessels

Vessels

A Program for Developing
Godly Eating Habits

Elyse Fitzpatrick, M.A.

UNCOMMON VESSELS
Copyright @ 1990 by Elyse Fitzpatrick

ISBN-10: 1-889032-27-1
ISBN-13: 978 -1-889032-27-6

Printed in the United States of America.

First printing 2001; Second printing 2003;
Third printing 2007; Fourth printing 2008

Dedication

To George and Eileen Scipione
examples of true godliness

Acknowledgement

Special thanks must be expressed to the heroic leaders of the biblical counseling movement that have shaped my thinking and encouraged my endeavors. Outstanding among these are Jay Adams, George Scipione, David Powlison, Bob Smith, and Steve Viars. My sincere thanks also go to all the hundreds of women who have worked through the Uncommon Vessels program and made it what it is today, especially the members of Faith Baptist Church in Lafayette, Indiana. Thanks also to Dave Crawley and Kim Monroe at TIMELESS TEXTS for their willingness to take on this project. May God be glorified in our lives.

Contents

Introduction
Finding God's Help

"I hope you can help me." The young woman sadly hung her head and folded her hands in front of her. "I've never weighed this much and I just can't seem to stop eating. I know that the Lord loves me and I really do love Him also, but since my husband and I have become Christians, it seems that I just can't control my eating. We used to do other things – drugs and stuff – and now all I can think about is what I'm going to eat next. You've got to help me. My husband is on my case all the time and my mother won't leave me alone. I hate the way I look and I know that my eating is out of control ... I've tried dieting, but my self-control doesn't last till lunch. What am I going to do? None of my clothes fit, I hate coming to church because I know I look so terrible in my tight dresses, and I refuse to go to any of the church fellowship meetings because it seems like all they do is eat, and I'm embarrassed to eat in front of people. I know that they must be thinking that I shouldn't eat anything, but what can I do? Can you help me?"

Does this story sound familiar to you? Since you've picked up this *Uncommon Vessels Member's Manual*, I'm assuming that you may have thought or said something similar to this. What I want to say to you is that there is hope. It isn't hope that will be found in this book or even in the group you may be joining. No, real hope is found in God and in His changeless Word. If you are His child, the God Who knows and loves you personally has committed Himself to your sanctification – that is, to your change into the likeness of Christ. Think about what He's said in Philippians 1:6, "*For I am* confident of this very thing, that He who began a good work in you will perfect it until the day of Christ Jesus." Just as Paul was confident that God was able and committed to changing His children, so you too can be confident. Think about this: God wants you to change more than you do – and for all the right reasons!

As you work through this manual, you'll discover biblical truths that will transform your life. You'll discover God's plan and method for your change, His pattern for developing godly eating habits, and some of the sinful habit patterns that you may have developed.

This program probably isn't like other "weight loss" programs you've been on. That's because the goal of this program isn't mere weight loss. No, the goal of this program is something far superior to the fleeting joy of fitting into your jeans. The goal of this program is that your eating be done for God's glory. That's what Paul taught in 1 Corinthians 10:31, "Whether, then, you eat or drink or whatever you do, do all to the glory of God."

Since the goal of the program isn't mere weight loss, the methods for accomplishing this goal are different as well. I'm not going to tell you that you should eat only grapefruit for 8 weeks. In fact, I'm not even going to tell you what you should or shouldn't eat at all! I want you (and your leaders, if you're in a group) to discover a good, nutritious diet (such as the American Heart Association Diet), that you can live with for the rest of your life. You see, the point of this program is to help you develop godly eating habits that will stick with you long after you've finished these Bible studies. If you're like most of us, you probably have a shelf in your library full of diet books. These diet books come and go, but our hearts aren't changed, so when we're finished with the "diet," we go right back to our old ways of eating. This program has been crafted to impact your inner man – your heart. It's my prayer that God's Spirit will use His Word to work in your heart through this program so that you'll find true victory in His power.

Another facet of this program is spiritual disciplines such as prayer, Bible reading, study, and fellowship. If you're in a group, you'll find great comfort and strength in the prayer and fellowship with others who are struggling with these issues.

If you're not in a formal group, why not ask a few friends or family members to help you by holding you accountable, or even studying with you? Ask the Lord to help you find someone you can partner with in this journey. Although it is recommended that these resources be used in a group setting, you can go through these studies alone, using the *Uncommon Vessels Leader's Manual*.[1]

Whether you're going it alone or with a group, why not begin today to ask our loving Father to work a new expectation and freedom in your heart? I know that you can change – because we serve a God Who loves to transform us for His glory!

---

1. Or, you can purchase my book, *Love to Eat, Hate to Eat* (Harvest House, 1999), which is geared to individual study.

A Biblical Perspective

What follows is a biblical discussion of food, dieting and the common problems that seem to trouble those of us who struggle with eating. In the following section I'll answer questions such as: "What does the Bible have to say about food and eating?" "Does the Word give us the acumen we need as we consider this subject?" "What is going on in the heart and life of those who falter in this area?"

As a sweep is made of the Bible, we find many references to both appropriate and inappropriate eating, which we will list by topic.

Created by God and Good

> Then God said, "Behold, I have given you every plant yielding seed that is on the surface of all the earth, and every tree which has fruit yielding seed; it shall be food for you; and to every beast of the earth and to every bird of the sky and to every thing that moves on the earth which has life, I have given every green plant for food"; and it was so. And God saw all that He had made and behold it was very good (Genesis 1:29–31a).

Given as a Gift by God

> "Every moving thing that is alive shall be food for you; I give all to you, as *I gave* the green plant" (Genesis 9:3).

(See also – Job 36:31; Psalm 111:5, 136:25, 145:15; Proverbs 30:8; Isaiah 3:1; Acts 14:17; 1 Timothy 4:3–5.)

> He causes the grass to grow for the cattle, and vegetation for the labor of man, so that he may bring forth food from the earth, and wine which makes man's heart glad, so that he may make his face glisten with oil, and food which sustains man's heart (Psalm 104:14–15).

> But she said, "As the LORD your God lives, I have no bread, only a handful of flour in the bowl and a little oil in the jar; and behold, I am gathering a few sticks that I may go in and prepare for me and my son, that we may eat it and die" (1 Kings 17:12).

1

"If we say, 'We will enter the city,' then the famine is in the city and we shall die there; and if we sit here, we die also…" (2 Kings 7:4a).

(See also Judges 19:5, 8; Genesis 18:5.)

Not Singularly Essential for Spiritual Life

But He answered and said, "It is written, 'MAN SHALL NOT LIVE ON BREAD ALONE, BUT ON EVERY WORD THAT PROCEEDS OUT OF THE MOUTH OF GOD'" (Matthew 4:4).

Do not be carried away by varied and strange teachings; for it is good for the heart to be strengthened by grace, not by foods, through which those who were thus occupied were not benefited (Hebrews 13:9).

And He said to His disciples, "For this reason I say to you, do not be anxious for *your* life, *as to* what you shall eat; nor for your body, *as to* what you shall put on. For life is more than food, and the body than clothing" (Luke 12:22–23).

Food was Resisted to Demonstrate Obedience and Integrity

And after He had fasted forty days and forty nights, He then became hungry. And the tempter came and said to Him, "If You are the Son of God, command that these stones become bread." But He answered and said, "It is written, 'MAN SHALL NOT LIVE ON BREAD ALONE, BUT ON EVERY WORD THAT PROCEEDS OUT OF THE MOUTH OF GOD'" (Matthew 4:2–4).

Then all the people came to persuade David to eat bread while it was still day; but David vowed saying, "May God do so to me, and more also, if I taste bread or anything else before the sun goes down." Now all the people took note *of it*, and it pleased them, just as everything the king did pleased all the people (2 Samuel 3:35–36).

(See also 2 Samuel 12:17, Daniel 1. For the antithesis, see Saul in 1 Samuel 28:23 and Saul and Jonathan in 1 Samuel 14:1-52.)

Used by Satan to Tempt to Sin

In Genesis 3 Adam and Eve are tempted to eat of the Tree of the Knowledge of Good and Evil by the serpent. And in Matthew 4:3

Satan tempts Jesus to turn stones into bread for His consumption after a forty day fast.

Withheld by God as a Judgement for Disobedience

"You shall sow much seed to the field but you shall gather in little, for the locusts shall consume it. You shall plant and cultivate vineyards, but you shall neither drink of the wine nor gather *the grapes*, for the worm shall devour them ... So all these curses shall come on you and pursue you and overtake you until you are destroyed, because you would not obey the LORD your God by keeping His commandments and His statutes which He commanded you (Deuteronomy 28:38–39, 45).

(See also Deuteronomy 28:51–57; Jeremiah 19:8–9.)

Promised to God's Covenant People

Blessed *shall be* the offspring of your body and the produce of your ground and the offspring of your beasts, the increase of your herd and the young of your flock. Blessed *shall be* your basket and your kneading bowl.
(Deuteronomy 28:4–5)

"Do not be anxious then, saying, 'What shall we eat?' or 'What shall we drink?' or 'With what shall we clothe ourselves?' For all these things the Gentiles eagerly seek; for your heavenly Father knows that you need all these things. But seek first His kingdom and His righteousness; and all these things shall be added to you" (Matthew 6:31–33).

"Consider the ravens, for they neither sow nor reap; and they have no storeroom nor barn; and *yet* God feeds them; how much more valuable you are than the birds!" (Luke 12:24).

To Be Received with Thanksgiving

... *men* who forbid marriage *and advocate* abstaining from foods, which God has created to be gratefully shared in by those who believe and know the truth. For everything created by God is good, and nothing is to be rejected, if it is received with gratitude (I Timothy 4:3–4).

(See also Romans 14:6, 1 Corinthians 10:30.)

Gluttony Related to Other Sins

> "And they shall say to the elders of his city, 'This son of ours is stubborn and rebellious, he will not obey us, he is a glutton and a drunkard.' Then all the men of his city shall stone him to death; so you shall remove the evil from your midst, and all Israel shall hear of *it* and fear.
> (Deuteronomy 21:20–21)

> Do not be with heavy drinkers of wine, *or* with gluttonous eaters of meat; for the heavy drinker and the glutton will come to poverty, and drowsiness will clothe *a man* with rags (Proverbs 23:20–21).

> "And do not seek what you shall eat, and what you shall drink, and do not keep worrying" (Luke 12:29).

> "Be on guard, that your hearts may not be weighted down with dissipation and drunkenness and the worries of life, and that day come on you suddenly like a trap..." (Luke 21:34).

> ...whose end is destruction, whose god is *their* appetite, and *whose* glory is in their shame, who set their minds on earthly things (Philippians 3:19).

(See also Proverbs 28:7, Luke 12:16–21, Numbers 11:4–6, 1 Samuel 2:12–17, 4:18, Genesis 25:30–34.)

Laws on Types of Food Allowed

Leviticus outlines many types of laws which were given under the old covenant not concerning the amounts of food to be eaten (except in the case of manna where a certain amount to be gathered was specified: as much as could be consumed in one day), but concerning the types of food to be eaten. These laws were revised by the apostles in Acts 15:20 after the Jerusalem council; the only restrictions were that they should abstain from things strangled and from eating meat with the blood.

In 1 Corinthians 10 and Romans 14 Paul discusses the morality of eating meat sacrificed to idols. The basic premise was that a person could eat anything for which his conscience didn't condemn him and which didn't cause his brother to stumble. Simply put, any eating of anything (actually any action taken at any time) should be done for, and to, the glory of God.

Food Was Offered to God as a Sacrifice

The Levitical offerings included cattle, sheep, fowl, grain, and fruit. The priests were recompensed with part of these offerings as a type of payment for services. In this agricultural society, the people were offering to God that which would sustain their lives.

Jesus Prepared Food, Ate With His Disciples, Performed Miracles With Food

> When He was at the table with them, He took bread, gave thanks, broke it and began to give it to them (Luke 24:30, NIV).

> And while they still did not believe it because of joy and amazement, he asked them, "Do you have anything here to eat?" They gave him a piece of broiled fish, and he took it and ate it in their presence (Luke 24:41–43, NIV).

> When they landed, they saw a fire of burning coals there with fish on it, and some bread.... Jesus said to them, "Come and have breakfast"... (John 21:9, 12, NIV).

Also, in Luke 9:10–17 Jesus feeds the five thousand. And in Luke 22 Jesus prepared the Last Supper and shared it with His disciples as He instituted communion.

ROOT SINS

When we examine the general area of gluttony closely, we can see that there are several areas of "root sins" that may attend this problem. In the following paragraphs, we will discuss these deeply ingrained behaviors, ways to deal with them, and Scripture that demonstrates and applies to these problems.

The first area for discussion is that of idolatry, or the worship of a false god. God's children are commanded in Exodus 20:3–5 to have "no other gods," and although no one actually worships or prays to food (not commonly at least), there is a definite connection between the need for communion with God and peace with Him and the satiating of that need with food. When anxious or fearful, you may eat instead of praying or waiting on God. Philippians 3:19 is a very interesting verse in this regard, "...whose end is destruction, whose god is *their* appetite, and *whose* glory is their shame, who set their minds on earthly things." The Greek word for appetite is "koilia," meaning "a hollow, a cavity, fig. the heart,"[1] and was metaphorically used for the innermost part of man (see John 7:38). These people had made a god out of their innermost desires. The emptiness within them and the desire to satiate this "appetite" was foremost in their lives. When you are experiencing emptiness and feel the desire to eat uncontrollably, you need to understand that you must put God first, rely on His strength, and feed on Him. Along these same lines is the Matthew 4 passage about being sustained by "every Word from the mouth of God." Ask yourself, "What am I feeling?" and "Do I feel true physical hunger or some sort of empty restlessness which is a craving for something other than food?" The Word is plain in Deuteronomy 6:4 and Matthew 22:36–38 that our love and devotion belong to God – heart, soul, mind, and BODY.

The second area of intensive concentration is that of a false savior. Although you, as a believing woman, know Christ as the Savior from sin, you may not know Him as Savior from present sins or the answer to every difficulty. In Matthew 11:28–29, Jesus calls to the weary and heavy laden with the promise of rest. You may experience weariness, or a burdening with the cares of life, or even self-righteousness. The Lord calls to you who are struggling under these loads and promises to give rest; however, you may still be trying to bear these burdens yourself. And when you find it too difficult, you may resort to compensatory eating, instead of coming to Christ. Psalm 16:11 tells us that in the presence of the Lord are pleasures and joys eternal. The flimsy and futile attempt to obtain pleasure from food, especially sweets, is frustrating at best. You must be taught reliance on the righteousness of Christ (which we will discuss in full) and reliance upon His joys and pleasures instead of food.

A note of caution should be given here about replacing this compensatory eating with any other compensatory behavior – including positive ones like exercise or hobbies. Although exercise and hobbies are both good, the proper course of action is prayer and reliance on Christ through support of other Christians, Bible reading, and learning to trust solely in Him to met all your needs.

A third area, that of control, also must be addressed. When you are experiencing frustrations over uncontrollable things in your life, you may justify your indulgence in food by petulantly stating, "I always have to do what other people tell me to do. All of my time is taken up in meeting the demands of others so when it comes to eating

---

1. James Strong, *Strong's Exhaustive Concordance* (Nashville: Crusade Bible Publishers, Inc.), p. 42.

NO ONE IS GOING TO TELL ME WHAT TO DO." You must be made to see that every area of your life belongs to Christ and that you must bow the knee to Him "...even in *this*" (Philippians 2:10–11). So start now by noting areas in your life in which you still desire control and then give them to the Lord. Romans 6:16 reads, "Do you not know that when you present yourselves to someone as slaves for obedience, you are slaves of the one whom you obey, either of sin resulting in death, or of obedience resulting in righteousness?" You must learn to become the "slave" of Jesus in every area of your life, and that you may not withhold anything from Him, nor should you want to.

Another root area is that of self-righteousness – the prideful desire to be "good enough" or perfect without God's help or in self-generated efforts. The New Testament is full of references to the righteousness of the believer resting in the righteousness of the Son. Philippians 3:9 states, "...and may be found in Him, not having a righteousness of my own derived from *the* Law, but that which is through faith in Christ, the righteousness which *comes* from God on the basis of faith...," and is particularly helpful in at least two relevant instances. The first is the "I can handle this problem on my own" attitude. You may refuse to get help for this problem or even to pray about it, since you feel like you can take care of it without help. The second instance is when you are doing very well on the program and starts to feel like you are really loved and accepted by God since you have this area under control now. But you must understand that your right-standing before God rests solely on the work of the cross and the obedience of Christ. A passage which is particularly beneficial in this regard is Hebrews 13:9: "Do not be carried away by varied and strange teachings; for it is good for the heart to be strengthened by grace, not by foods, through which those who were thus occupied were not benefited." The meaning of this passage is that eating special foods does not profit in terms of justification, cleansing of the conscience, or sanctification. Only grace–the free, unmerited favor of a merciful God – can bring strength and establish or confirm your heart. You can stand in the presence of God with boldness, not because you have kept to your diet successfully, but because God, in His mercy, has chosen you and redeemed you.

FRUIT SINS

Stemming from the above areas are numerous "fruit sins," or results of this kind of wrong thinking and acting. These areas include vain concern about outward appearances, worry and anxiety, boredom and loneliness, lack of self-control in many other areas including speech, dishonesty or deceitful behaviors, self-centeredness, and a thankless attitude.

You need to understand that God looks on the inward heart – the motivations and intentions – along with the outward actions. There are no verses that teach that we need to look thin, but there are many references to God's searching the innermost being, including Jeremiah 17:10: "I, the Lord, search the heart, I test the mind, even to give to each man according to his ways, according to the results of his deeds." The Lord is concerned with the inner man being made beautiful: "And let not your adornment be *merely* external – braiding the hair, and wearing gold jewelry, or putting on dresses; but *let it be* the hidden person of the heart, the imperishable quality of a gentle and quiet spirit, which is precious is the sight of God" (1 Peter 3:3–4). Some of you may have been dealing with your weight problem for so long that you may use it to excuse yourself from dealing with or facing other more glaring sins. God is concerned about every facet of your life – not just weight – and wants to "sanctify them wholly; spirit, soul and body" (I Thessalonians 5:23).

In several places Jesus lumped together a lifestyle of intemperance and worry. He also admonished his followers on several occasions not to worry about food or clothing.

Many women confess that their overeating is done to soothe themselves when worrying about some particular problem – sometimes even in response to free-floating anxiety. In Luke 21:34, the Lord tells us to "Be on guard, that your hearts may not be weighted down with dissipation and drunkenness and the worries of life, and that day come on you suddenly like a trap..." Worry and a lack of discipline feed on each other. Perhaps you are concerned and anxious over your husband's job or your own job. So you eat and let down your discipline, which gives temporary pleasure but soon causes more worry about gaining weight and being out of control, which then causes more eating, and so on. You must learn to cast your cares on the Lord, since He truly cares for you. When you are worried and tempted to eat, call someone in your support group for prayer and strength.

Many severely obese women suffer from boredom and loneliness; at times this loneliness and boredom is engendered by the weight problem itself. They hate the way they look, they won't or can't participate in sports, they feel conspicuous at events where food is served (believing that everyone is watching how much or what they eat) and so they stay home and eat to soothe their need for fellowship and normal friendly relationships. If this is the case, even before you have lost your weight, you must be reassured that your life belongs to Christ. Even if you feel useless or out of place, you must frequently spend some time in service to God and others. Make a list of your gifts and areas of usefulness in your congregation. After looking at 2 Samuel 11:1–4, note how staying at home away from the battle was the beginning of many other sinful and destructive behaviors. The point again is NOT to merely fill your life with some other compulsive, compensatory behavior, but to get involved in serving Christ and His body.

James 3:2 tells us, "For we all stumble in many *ways*. If anyone does not stumble in what he says, he is a perfect man, able to bridle the whole body as well." Another area of disciplining the body is in our speech. You may be a compulsive overeater who has problems here also (following along with the general lack of discipline) including lying, exaggerating, gossiping, putting others down, or faithless speech. You need to pinpoint problem areas and with continual reliance on the Lord learn to rehabituate your speech patterns. Ephesians 4:29–32 tells us what types of speech to put off and what types to put on. Remember that it isn't enough to just stop lying, you must become a truth teller.

Along with lying, the general category of honesty should be addressed. Some women have a long history of sneaking food and covering up problems. A woman may even have deceived herself into thinking that she really doesn't over-eat and really does exercise as much as others. Of course, there may be medical problems which play into this and the help of a physician should be elicited. But the general lying to oneself must be confronted. That is why it is necessary to keep a careful record of all food eaten in what amounts and all exercise completed. That way you can really see where your problems lie. Of course, you may be dishonest with your record-keeping, and the scale may bear that out over a course of time. Your lying and covering-up is part of the "old nature" addressed in Colossians 3:9, "Do not lie to one another, since you laid aside the old self with its *evil* practices."

Almost all Christians must be continually reminded to live sacrificially to God. We all have a bent to live selfishly and to demand that things go our own way. If you are motivated solely by weight loss and not by godliness or sacrifice to God, the first time a gain on the scale is registered, you may become seriously discouraged and quit. Godly motivation and sacrificial living must be at the core of any spiritual discipline program, or it is doomed to failure. The failure isn't only in not losing weight; even if weight is lost, if it is done for self-centered reasons, the fruit of this action will not be eternal or bring glory to God. Romans 12:1 and Acts 20:24 are helpful here, along with 1 Corinthians 6:20: "For you have been bought with a price: therefore glorify God in your body."

All Christians should spend time specifying the wonders of God in their lives. So you should give thanks to God, especially at any significant accomplishment or insight. You should also give thanks according to 1 Timothy 4:4, "For everything created by God is good, and nothing is to be rejected, if it is received with gratitude," for *everything* you eat – *before* you eat it. Aside from the point of Biblical obedience, you will also have to stop momentarily and bring the Lord into the situation. Colossians 2:6–7 tells us to walk in the Lord, being built up in Him and overflowing with gratitude.

One more area which needs illumination at this point is that of the deceptiveness and the hardening entanglement which is the nature of sin. Our flesh loves the enslaving effect of sin, and we are constantly having to fight against our flesh. We need to be reminded about the deceptiveness – the feeling that everything is really okay, the idea that God doesn't really care – that accompanies sin. So you must make the conscious effort not to be hardened against the conviction of the Holy Spirit as Hebrews 3:13 states, "But encourage one another day after day, as long as it is *still* called 'Today'; lest any one of you be hardened by the deceitfulness of sin." In order to prevent this hardening, you need to learn to repent and confess your sins. Accepting or glossing over sins, rather than confessing them is the sure way to become hardened to the Lord's working in an area. I John 1:8–9 reads, "If we say that we have no sin, we are deceiving ourselves, and the truth is not in us. If we confess our sins, He is faithful and righteous to forgive our sins and to cleanse us from unrighteousness." You should learn to acknowledge points of disobedience and sin and must confess and repent of them, asking and accepting forgiveness. The repentance involves a change in behavior – more than saying "I'm sorry" – a true effort must be made to change actions and even motivations, all the time relying on the grace and strength of the Lord.

From the previous brief outline we can discern that food and the process of eating is good and pleasurable and given to sustain life. We also understand that, like any of God's gifts, food can be abused, and this abusing constitutes sin. We know that Satan hates it when we use the pleasurable things that God has given us appropriately, and he will use food to undermine our relationship with God whenever he can.

If there is any one overriding rule about how to eat in a way that pleases God, it has to be that of self-discipline. Although Paul knew that he had the liberty to eat meat sacrificed to idols, he also exercised self-control for the sake of the Kingdom. 1 Corinthians 9:27 teaches us that he "buffeted his body," he "made it his slave." Paul wasn't concerned about his liberty to eat a brownie; no, he was concerned about any enslaving behavior that would thwart his ministry. Although the Bible doesn't specify any particular diet as more godly than another, some basic principles are given so that we may learn to judge our eating habits. I've compiled these principles into an acrostic "D-I-S-C-I-P-L-I-N-E-D E-ating." The 12 letters in this acrostic stand for 12 questions that you can learn to ask yourself before eating anything. Although this may seem overwhelming at the beginning, once these principles have been learned, they will become second nature. Each one is covered in a Bible study later in the course, but you should be acquainted with them as soon as possible.

The Program

Uncommon Vessels (UV) as presented here has been tailored for a small group setting. At our church, we run several groups consisting of ten to twelve people. The groups are moderated by women who have been successful in the program. These groups meet once a week for 12 weeks and follow all the disciplines as laid out in the program.

You may tailor this program to fit – either on a personal one-to-one level or in groups as we have.

The following divisions of the program consist of general guidelines about UV, Bible studies for the members, Bible discussion guides for the leaders (topics taken from the above areas of need), and various forms. There is no diet included. You can use any reasonable diet program, such as the American Diabetes Association Diet or American Heart Association Diet.

Each member should be strongly encouraged to seek medical advice before going on any diet or taking up any strenuous exercise program. It would be a good idea to let her physician or dietician design a diet suited especially for her.

If you are going to run this program in group fashion, an Orientation Meeting with mandatory attendance is suggested. During this evening, outline the goals of the program and how this program would be different from a Weight Watchers type of meeting. Specify the times and dates for the program (See Orientation Outline). Let the prospective members consider their commitment for one week before signing-up, when they should bring with them a signed Contract of Commitment.

REQUIRED DISCIPLINES

For the moment, all discipline seems painful rather than pleasant; later it yields the peaceful fruit of righteousness to those who have been trained by it (Hebrews 12:11, RSV).

It is God's desire that your life would reflect His character by being well-ordered and disciplined. The disciplines of the *Uncommon Vessels* program will serve as tools to draw you closer to Him in several areas of your life. These areas include learning proper eating habits, establishing a consistent prayer time and daily Bible reading, and developing genuine care for others. Each discipline is an important and necessary part of UV's goal to help you become the person God wants you to be – one who truly glorifies Him in your entire life. It is my desire that this program would be a vehicle that God would use to change not only the visible, outward man, but also the inner, hidden motivations and intentions of the heart.

Your co-leaders and the group coordinator are committed to being your servants during this special training time. They are going to seek to encourage you and help you carry out your commitment. You can facilitate this training by allowing God to speak to you through them.

*Below you will find a list of the disciplines
required in this program.*

Weekly Attendance	Controlled Eating
Menu & Daily Diary	Weekly Weigh-In
Memory Verse	Goal Setting
Prayer	Bible Reading
Bible Study	Phone Calls
Exercise	

Weekly Attendance

Part of your commitment to the Uncommon Vessels program is attendance at each meeting. These meetings last only one hour, and your attendance is very important for several reasons. First, if you are discouraged and think that you might possibly have a weight gain, it is very important to come to class to be encouraged again and not give up. Your attendance is also important for the other women in the group – perhaps they are struggling with the same things that you are and will be encouraged by you. This is your time for prayer and fellowship; don't let any distraction come between you and your commitment to become disciplined for God's glory.

Controlled Eating

No matter what particular diet you choose to follow, if you are just going to eat a certain number of calories or fat grams, or if you are going to target a specific style of eating, you need to find a diet that is healthy and that will fit easily into your lifestyle.

Some of us do better with detailed strategies, while others of us know enough about how to eat properly that we really don't need anyone to tell us. You make the decision. Remember, though, that you can always change your mind. If you discover that you can't stay focused without a specific diet, then go ahead and use one.

General Guidelines

If you are seeking to lose weight, and you need help determining how many calories you might want to eat, then multiply your healthy goal weight by 9 or 10 (for women) or 11 to 13 (for men). For instance, if a healthy weight for you is approximately 150 pounds, you can multiply that by 9 (9 X 150), which equals 1350. This is the total number of calories you can eat to maintain (or achieve) a weight of 150. If you consistently, over a long period of time, eat 1350 calories per day, you will probably continue to lose weight until you reach your goal.

Let's assume that the number of calories you should eat on a daily basis is 1350. You can take 1200 of these calories and divide them up between the three most calorie-rich food sources: Carbohydrates, proteins, and fat. Of these, you should spend no more than 60% or 720 calories on carbohydrates, which include breads, starches, pastas, and cereals. Fifteen percent of your calories (180) should be allotted to proteins which would include all meats and soybean products. (Remember that high fat meats have more calories, so you'll have to eat smaller portions of them to stay within your percentages.) Fat, which includes butter, margarine, salad dressings, animal and vegetable oils, should account for no more than 25% or 300 calories. You can split the remaining 150 calories between dairy products, fruits and vegetables (which are generally very low in calories). This formula is very simplistic, however, and doesn't take into account the differences in body mass (fat/muscle mass) or the amount of exercise you're doing. Your physician or nutritionist would be the best resource for you to consult as you plan a healthy eating program. In any case, you need to notify your group leader about your choice of diet.

Whether you choose to use a specific diet (such as the American Heart Association Diet) or just want to monitor your calories, fat grams, or certain types of foods, you will need to indicate whether your eating is truly disciplined according to biblical standards. Remember that you may be able to eat all the food allowed on a certain plan and still not have the change of heart that this program is focused on. What follows is an acrostic that will help you learn principles for biblical eating, and it would be beneficial for you to commit these questions to memory as soon as possible. On your daily diary is a section marked with a "D" at the top. This is where you are to record your struggles with these principles, as shown in the sample (see "Completed Daily Diary," page 92).

D-I-S-C-I-P-L-I-N-E-D Eating Questions

Doubt: Do I doubt (for whatever reason) that I can eat this food without sinning?

Idolatry: Will eating this food demonstrate a heart of idolatry (pleasure/power)?

Stumble: If I eat this food will it cause some weaker Christian to stumble?

Covet: Am I eating this food because I saw someone else with it and I'm coveting?

Inroad: If I eat this food will it create an inroad for sin in my life?

Praise: Can I eat this food with thanks and gratitude?

Life: Would eating this food harm my life or health in any way?

Illustrate: Am I modeling good eating habits for others?

No: Am I able to say "no" to this food, even if I know that I can eat it without sin?

Emotions: Does the desire to eat this food flow out of any sinful emotion?

Distract: Will preparing or eating this food distract me from something more profitable?

Enslaved: Will eating this food bring me under any kind of bondage?

In my eating and drinking, am I glorifying God?

On your daily diary, under the category headed with a "D," indicate the first letter (or letters) of the question you violated when you ate a particular food or in a particular way. For instance, if you knew that you shouldn't have eaten that extra cookie, even though you had enough calories left in the day to do so, you should record a "N" for the word "No." You could have eaten the food without sinning in any way, but you knew that you should have practiced self-discipline, and so you violated that principle. This may seem confusing right now, but as you work through the Bible studies on these questions, these principles will become more clear. Just remember that you're growing in the practice of self-discipline, so you may struggle for a time.

Menu and Daily Diary

If you are desiring to learn to control your eating, you will be recording *everything* you eat on your menu sheet, no matter what type of diet you choose. It is of utmost importance that you be honest. These menus will be turned in to your leader during your weigh-in time every week. Your leaders will evaluate your menu and return it to you the following week. This is an important part of the program and will help teach you godly eating habits. Even if you are not trying to lose weight and therefore are not recording your food choices, you will still be required to record your daily spiritual disciplines.

How to Complete the Menu and Daily Diary

Record everything you eat after each meal. For your convenience, the menu is divided into food groups. Record either the number of fat grams, the number of calories, or the number of food exchanges in the appropriate square, according to your specific diet.

Write the *exact type* of food and the *exact size* of the serving next to the number of grams, calories, or exchanges.

Record both your areas of victory and needed growth in the appropriate square. If you find that you've been able to resist that extra helping, then record that. If, on the other hand, you weren't able to resist, record that also. At the end of the week you'll have a clear record of the areas you've grown in and those you may need to focus on for the next week. You should weigh and measure your food exactly. In order to do this, you can buy a scale and remember to use it at every meal!

Your water intake, prayer time, Bible reading, and exercise should also be recorded in your diary.

Bible Study

Each week answer the questions in the personal Bible study that you received from your leader. These studies and questions are designed to help you understand and apply scriptural truths to your life. Do the Bible study at the beginning of the week. Your leader will check to be sure that you have completed it at the beginning of the class each week.

Bible Reading

Daily Bible reading is an important part of your spiritual growth. You should seek to discover the truth that you don't "live by bread alone, but by every word that proceeds from the mouth of God" (Matthew 4:4, Deuteronomy 8:3b). You should strive to read two chapters in the Bible each day. You should read consecutively through the book of your choice, either Old or New Testament, and your daily readings are to be recorded on your diary.

Memory Verse

Each Bible study indicates a specific verse for you to memorize for that week. These verses will help you resist temptation and will encourage you in the disciplines of the program. You should strive to memorize the verse at the beginning of the week, and you will recite it to your leader at weigh-in.

Phone Call

Make one phone call to a member of your group each week. This can be a great time for sharing and praying for one another. Be considerate of the time and length of the phone call, however. You will be given a list with all the members' phone numbers. Record the name of the person you called in your diary in the "Victories" portion of your diary.

Prayer

Nothing will cause your spiritual growth like consistent daily prayer. Pray for each member in your group each day. Make an effort to pray at about the same time each day, if possible.

- Try to make your prayer time exclusive.
- Record the time of prayer in your diary each day.
- Prayer requests will be taken at the end of each meeting.

Prayer Before Eating

Before eating any food, stop and give thanks for it. First Thessalonians 4:4–5 teaches that you are to receive food with gratitude and prayer. These few moments to become thankful will become a true source of blessing and strength for you, especially when you are tempted to eat something wrong.

Exercise

Exercise is one of the two great keys to weight loss (and general good health). Regular exercise raises your metabolic rate so that you will naturally burn more calories (even when you're not exercising) than a person who doesn't exercise. If regular exercise is not presently part of your lifestyle, *start slowly* with walking. Below you will find a list of calories per hour burned (on average). Try to spread your exercise out evenly over the week – three shorter times are better than one longer time. You should try to burn around 1,000 calories in exercise per week. Record your specific exercise and approximate caloric burn on your diary. The following averages are based on a 150 pound person. Calories burned per hour:

- 300 – golf (walking), tennis, racquetball, walking (3 miles per hour), aerobics, bicycling, calisthenics, dancing, cross-country skiing
- 400 – competitive tennis
- 500 – swimming (per mile)
- 600 – exercycle (high intensity)

Goal Setting

At the beginning of each UV session, you will be asked to set goals for yourself. If you are trying to lose weight, then you should indicate the amount of weight you would like to lose over the next 12 weeks. Remember that a loss of 1 pound per week is good and that you aren't losing muscle or just water with that kind of loss. If you aren't looking to lose weight specifically, but just want to develop a more disciplined lifestyle, then indicate in what areas you want to work on your goal setting sheet.

In our groups, we ask that each member place a total of $75 into this goal fund agreement. This money may be collected at the first meeting, or over the 12 weeks of the course. This money will be refunded at the end of the session to those who have completed the course and achieved their goal. It will be more difficult to judge whether or not those who have set spiritual goals have completed these goals, but if you think that you have, then your leader will refund your money. Of course, at the least, completing your goal would necessitate your finishing the entire session. For those who do not achieve their goals, or those who drop out, the $75 will be sent to the mission project of your choice. It is not the policy of UV to profit from goal setting, so any left over money will be used for missionary projects only. Any person who is dropped from the group for non-attendance will forfeit their money to mission projects. If the $25 per month would be too much of a strain on your family, talk with your leader about an amount that you could afford. Remember, this goal fund is for your motivation.

You will also be given a commitment card on which you can write any other personal goals that you might have. These cards will be kept for you, unopened, until the last meeting, when they will be returned to you.

Water Intake

Whatever eating option you choose, you will be asked to consume *64 ounces of water per day*. If you are not accustomed to drinking this much water, it will be difficult at first, but you will find that in a very short period of time, your body will be craving water. Your body retains or releases water according to your daily intake. In most cases, so little water is being ingested that your body retains more than is necessary. Interestingly, those who are changing their eating habits tend to lose more quickly and in greater quantities when water is consumed on a consistent, daily basis. Water also helps to suppress the appetite and helps to metabolize stored fat. It helps maintain proper muscle tone, which will facilitate your exercise program. It helps relieve the body of wastes and will help alleviate constipation. You may choose to follow this schedule:

Morning: 22 ounces consumed over a 30-minute period.
Noon: 22 ounces consumed over a 30-minute period.
Evening: 20 ounces consumed between five and six o'clock.

What's Your Motivation?

Whether, then, you eat or drink or whatever you do, do all to the glory of God (1 Corinthians 10:31).

Scripture: 2 Corinthians 5:9; Colossians 1:10; Hebrews 4:12

Let's take time now as we begin this session to think about our motives and to examine our hearts. Take time as you read these verses to pray for understanding and to ask the Lord to help you have godly motives, ones that He will bless.

1. As I look at my life, I see that I usually have the following reasons or motives:

2. As I think about UV in particular, I see that I have these motives:

3. After reading 2 Corinthians 5:9, I see that my ambition or goal ought to be:

4. As I seek to fulfill Colossians 1:10 this week, I will:

Hebrews 4:12 teaches that God's Word will expose the motives and intentions of our hearts. Write out a prayer for this week that the Lord would be pleased to give you insights into your own motives.

A Living Sacrifice

I urge you therefore, brethren, by the mercies of God, to present your bodies a living and holy sacrifice, acceptable to God, which is your spiritual service of worship (Romans 12:1).

Scripture: Mark 9:35; Matthew 23:11; Acts 20:24; 1 Corinthians 6:20

1. According to Romans 12:1, what is your spiritual service of worship?

2. What does the phrase "a living sacrifice" mean to you? What did it mean in the context of the Jewish sacrifices and ceremonies?

3. Mark 9:35 and Matthew 23:11 are similar in what ways?

4. Are you seeking to serve? In what ways?

5. What are the declarations that Paul made about his life in Acts 20:24?

6. What does it mean to "count your life as dear"? What might stop you from laying down your life in service to God?

7. First Corinthians 6:20 teaches that God makes a certain claim on your body. What is it?

8. What was the means of His purchasing you?

Everyday that we live is to be offered to God as a service and sacrifice to Him. Pray this week that you would be more aware of His desires for your life and would fulfill them.

All or Nothing – Satan's Tool for Failure

Not that I have already obtained it, or have already become perfect, but I press on in order that I may lay hold of that for which also I was laid hold of by Christ Jesus (Philippians 3:12).

Scripture: 1 John 1:8–10; Romans 2:28–29, Galatians 2:16, 20–21, 3:1–5, 5:11, 19–21

1. Striving to be "perfect" or "self-righteous" in your own abilities will usually lead to frustration and self-indulgence. What does 1 John 1:10 teach about our ability to be sinless?

2. As you consider your life, are there times that you are trying to be the "perfect little girl?" What are they?

3. According to Romans 2:28–29, where do true changes take place?

4. When you strive to be perfect in your own strength, what part of your life are you actually working on? Is this pleasing to Christ or your own pride?

5. Much of the book of Galatians is written to those who were saved by grace but were trying to become perfect by their works. After reading the above verses, try to boil down Paul's message into a sentence or two. What do you think he meant in 5:11 when he called the cross a "stumbling block"? Why would he list the works of the flesh in this context?

6. When we try to become sanctified or perfected by our works, what are we saying about the cross?

7. Did Paul attain perfection? According to Philippians 3:12, how should we live? What should we do when we sin?

Spend time praying this week that you would learn to rest in His completed work.

Be On Your Guard

Beware, and be on your guard against every form of greed; for not even *when one has an abundance does his life consist of his possessions* (Luke 12:15).

Scripture: Numbers 11:1–34; 1 Samuel 14:32–33;
Colossians 3:5, 8, 12–14; Luke 12:13–34

1. What happened to those who were dissatisfied with manna and wanted quail? (Numbers 11:1–34.) How does the Bible describe them?

2. In 1 Samuel 14:32–33, what happened to Saul's men when they were hungry? What was sinful about the way they had eaten?

3. Describe times when you have eaten in a sinful manner.

4. Are you usually content and thankful for the food you have? Are you remembering to thank God for it and to calm your heart before eating? What happens when you don't?

5. In Colossians 3:5, how does Paul define greed?

6. What does he advise that we do with greed? What should we "put on" instead of greed?

7. Is it possible to be thankful and content while being greedy? Why not?

8. In Luke 12:13–34, what are the things that Jesus tells us to seek after?

Spend time in prayer this week, praying that the main desire of your life would be for God and His kingdom. Confess the areas of your life where you have been greedy and ask the Lord to cleanse you and to create in you a thankful and contented heart instead.

Boredom and Loneliness

I press on toward the goal for the prize of the upward call of God in Christ Jesus (Philippians 3:14).

Scripture: Philippians 3:3–14; 2 Timothy 4:6–8; 2 Samuel 11:1–4

1. What decision had David made before he sinned with Bathsheba? (2 Samuel 11:1–4.) What should he have been doing?

2. Paul describes his life in what terms in 2 Timothy 4:6–8? What reward is he looking forward to?

3. Philippians 3:3–14 describe Paul's life goal in what terms?

4. What does the phrase "to know Christ" mean?

5. In what ways are you pressing on?

6. In what ways are you pouring out yourself for others?

7. List areas of service in your local church where your gifts are needed.

8. Name one friend who is outside your church whom you could disciple and help.

Ask God to show you concrete areas of service in which you could be involved this week.

Carried Away and Enticed

But each one is tempted when he is carried away and enticed by his own lust (James 1:14).

Scripture: 1 Thessalonians 3:5; James 1:13–17, 4:7;
I Corinthians 10:13; 2 Peter 2:9; Matthew 6:13

1. What does the word "lust" mean?

2. How do our lusts cause and play into our habitual sin?

3. In your life, what do you lust after? What are the desires that seem to drive you?

4. Who is it that tempts you to sin? (1 Thessalonians 3:5)

5. Who should we not blame? (James 1:13)

6. How does Satan tempt us?

7. What are the promises we have regarding temptation? (1 Corinthians 10:13; 2 Peter 2:9)

8. What is your part in the process of resisting temptation? (Matthew 6:13; James 4:7)

Spend time in prayer this week that the Lord would show you what your desires or lusts are and that He would deliver you from temptation.

Feeding On Christ

Jesus said to them, 'I am the bread of life; he who comes to Me shall not hunger, and he who believes in Me shall never thirst (John 6:35).

Scripture: Matthew 4:1–4, 5:6; Isaiah 55:1–3; John 6:1–40

1. After reading John 6, write in two or three sentences Jesus' teaching.

2. When Satan tempted Jesus to sinful eating in Matthew 4, what was our Lord's reply?

3. How does this truth relate to your progress in UV?

4. Can you think of others in Scripture who were tempted by sinful eating?

5. What does Isaiah 55:1–3 teach about the kind of nourishment that is truly valuable?

6. The next time you feel the emptiness that makes you want to eat sinfully, what should you do?

Spend time listening to the Lord this week through prayer, Bible reading, and fellowship. Ask Him to fill the longings of your heart with His purpose and presence.

Confession and Repentance

If we confess our sins, he is faithful and just to forgive us our sins, and to cleanse us from all unrighteousness (1 John 1:9, KJV).

Scripture: 1 John 1:5–10; Romans 10:9–10; Proverbs 28:13

1. Has the Lord revealed any sin in your thoughts, speech, or actions recently that needs to be confessed (acknowledged) and repented of (changed)?

2. What does 1 John 1:5–10 teach about those who say that they have no sin?

3. When are we able to have true fellowship with God and one another?

4. What does the phrase "walk in the light" mean?

5. Are there any areas in your life in which you know you're walking in darkness? What are they? What do you need to do about them?

6. What does Proverbs 28:13 teach about the person who confesses and forsakes his sin?

Spend time in prayers of confession and repentance this week. Try to focus on a specific area of weakness with which you know you struggle. Ask the Lord for His grace to make you strong against sin.

Controlling Your Tongue

For we all stumble in many ways. If anyone does not stumble in what he says, he is a perfect man, able to bridle the whole body as well (James 3:2).

Scripture: James 3:2–12; Ephesians 4:29–32; Proverbs 6:19; Numbers 13:25–14:3; Colossians 3:9

1. James 3 describes our tongues and speech in what word pictures?

2. As we strive to bridle our bodies, where should we start?

3. Ephesians 4:29–32 links speech with certain attitudes. What are they?

4. Proverbs 6:19 lists two types of speech God hates. What are they?

5. Numbers 13:25–14:3 describes the bad report brought back by the spies. What effect did their bad speech have on their brothers?

6. How important is your speech to your own success in life and in this program?

7. How important is your speech to the success of others?

8. What types of words should you practice saying?

Spend time this week praying about your speech and how it impacts others. Ask the Lord to help you control your tongue as you use it to build up others.

Developing a Correct Self-Image

For not he who commends himself is approved, but whom the Lord commends (2 Corinthians 10:18).

Scripture: Matthew 22:34–40, 23:5–7; Ephesians 2:4–8, 5:29;
Luke 9:23–24; 2 Timothy 3:1–5;
Philippians 2:3, 21, 3:3–4, 9; Romans 12:3;
2 Corinthians 10:12; Genesis 4:7

1. In our culture there has been a great emphasis on learning to love oneself. Some have even been taught that Jesus commanded us to do so in Matthew 22:28–40. What commands is Jesus giving in these verses?

2. What is the *implied assumption* in verse 39? List some of the ways that you love yourself.

3. According to Ephesians 5:29, how do we generally treat ourselves?

4. Since the Bible teaches that we already love ourselves too much, what should our attitude toward ourselves be?

    a. Luke 9:23–24

    b. Philippians 2:3

    c. Philippians 2:21

    d. Philippians 3:3–4, 9

    e. Romans 12:3

    f. 2 Corinthians 10:12

5. In your opinion, did the Pharisees have a problem with low self-esteem? What was their problem? (Matthew 23:5–7)

6. How does 2 Timothy 3:1–5 describe people in the last days? Does loving yourself more and more cause you to love others?

7. What does Ephesians 2:4–8 teach about God's mercy and our goodness?

8. As you evaluate yourself, do you think that you need to love yourself or God more?

9. In what areas of the program have you been loving and nourishing yourself too much?

10. God told Cain that he could "feel better" by doing what? (Genesis 4:7)

Spend time praying this week that God would enable you to love and serve Him more constantly. A burning heart of love stems from gratefulness for His mercy and grace.

Don't Be Fooled

But encourage one another day after day, as long as it is called "Today," lest any one of you be hardened by the deceitfulness of sin (Hebrews 3:13).

Scripture: Numbers 11:1–6; Hebrews 12:14–17; 1 Samuel 2:12–17; Proverbs 23:20

1. In what ways is sin "deceitful"?

2. How would you describe its hardening effects?

3. Numbers 11:4 describes the Israelites as greedy. In what ways were they greedy?

4. Hebrews 12:14–17 describes Esau as godless and immoral. Why?

5. 1 Samuel 2:12–17 tells us of the actions of the sons of Eli. What were they doing?

6. Proverbs 23:20 links what sins together?

7. Because sin is so deceptive and our flesh is so given to it, what must we do to ensure our continued walk with the Lord?

Spend time this week asking the Lord to reveal areas in your life where you are being deceived about the nature and danger of sin. When you are made aware of an area, take time right then to confess, repent, and plead with the Lord to change and protect you.

Honesty

...but speaking the truth in love, we are to grow up in all aspects *into Him...*(Ephesians 4:15).

Scripture: Ephesians 4:15, 25; Zechariah 8:16; Colossians 3:9

1. What does the phrase "speaking the truth in love" mean?

2. How is this concept tied into "growing up into Him"?

3. According to Ephesians 4:25, why should we speak the truth with each other?

4. Zechariah 8:16 tells us that speaking and judging in truth brings what blessing?

5. How does lying take your peace away?

6. Colossians 3:9 teaches that lying is a practice that belongs to whom?

7. List the areas that you have been dishonest in this program.

8. List the areas that you are generally dishonest in your life.

9. List the areas that you are generally dishonest with yourself.

10. What motivates you to be dishonest?

This week make a renewed effort to be honest with yourself, others and the Lord. Ask Him to show you the areas where you fail to love truth. When He does, repent and plead with Him for a changed heart.

Pressure or Stress – Your Choice

Yet those who wait for the LORD will gain new strength;
they will mount up with wings like eagles, they will run and
not get tired, they will walk and not become weary (Isaiah
40:31).

Scripture: Isaiah 40:27–31; Jeremiah 17:5–8; Philippians 4:10–13

1. As you reflect on your life, what are your typical areas of stress?

2. Was there ever a time when these stressful things were enjoyable to you? If so, what caused the change?

3. When you look at Isaiah 40:27–31, what factors seem to contribute to being weary or stressful?

4. In this passage, how does the Lord instruct you to handle weariness or lack of power?

5. Jeremiah 17:5–8 describes the difference between the person who trusts in mankind and the one who trusts in the Lord. Discuss what those differences are and what that means in your life.

6. Paul informs the Philippians that he learned the secret of contentment and peace. What was that secret?

As the week progresses, remember to ask the Lord to help you accomplish the tasks before you in His strength and with His help. Remember that He is mindful of you and that He has promised not to put anything in your path that you can't handle.

Living by the Word

Thy words were found and I ate them, and Thy words became for me a joy and the delight of my heart; for I have been called by Thy name, O LORD God of hosts (Jeremiah 15:16).

Scripture: Genesis 2:16-17; Matthew 4:1–4, 5:6; Jeremiah 15:16; John 4:34; Deuteronomy 8:3

1. What was the command that God gave to Adam and Eve in the garden? (Genesis 3:1–7)

2. In your opinion, what was God trying to teach Adam and Eve?

3. What was God teaching the Israelites as He fed them with manna in the wilderness? (Deuteronomy 8:3)

4. In Matthew 4:1–4 with what did Satan tempt Jesus?

5. How did the Lord respond?

6. Jeremiah speaks of "eating" God's word. What does he mean by this? Is this something that you could do?

7. Jesus speaks of food and hunger in John 4:34 and Matthew 5:6. What kind of hunger is He referring to?

8. Do you find yourself hungering for the Lord? Are you hungering for His kingdom or your own desires? Are you more like Adam and the Israelites or Jesus?

9. How can you fight the temptation to seek to satisfy yourself outside of Christ?

10. What parts does the Word play in your warfare against temptation and in satisfying your spiritual hunger?

Spend time praying this week that you would be satisfied with God's provision in Christ and that you wouldn't be tempted to satisfy your hunger outside of His will.

The Process of Biblical Change

...that, in reference to your former manner of life, you lay aside the old self...and...be renewed in the spirit of your mind, and put on the new self, which in the likeness of *God has been created in righteousness and holiness of the truth* (Ephesians 4:22–24).

Scriptures: Romans 6:11–14, 16–23; 12:1–2; Ephesians 4:22–32

1.   How do you think change occurs in a Christian's life?

2.   What is this action of change called?

3.   What does Romans 6:11–14 teach about sin in the believer's life?

4.   Are Christians sinless after conversion? Will there ever be a time when they will be?

5.   What does Paul mean when he says that Christians are "free from sin"?

6. What does Romans 12:1–2 teach about how to change?

7. What are the two facets of change discussed in Ephesians 4:22–32?

8. How is true Christian change different from other self-help programs?

9. How does the power of the Holy Spirit work in a believer's life?

10. What are the behaviors that Paul teaches should be put-off and put-on in Ephesians 4:22–32?

Spend time praying that the process of change – the putting off, putting on and renewing of the mind – will become clear to you. Although we frequently desire a quick fix, God is involved with us for the long haul. He is committed to change you, and the power of the Holy Spirit will accomplish this change. Pray that God would make you willing and obedient.

Sweet Speech – Our Goal

Let no unwholesome word proceed from your mouth, but only such a word *as is good for edification according to the need* of the moment, *that it may give grace to those who hear* (Ephesians 4:29).

Scripture: 1 Corinthians 10:10–13; Exodus 16:2–3, 8; Numbers 11:1;
Psalm 106:24–25

1. In 1 Corinthians 10:10–13 there is both a warning for grumbling and a promise in trial. Write them out in your own words.

2. Exodus 16:2–3, 8 refers to the Israelites as grumblers. Against whom were they actually grumbling? When we grumble and complain, who are we attacking?

3. Numbers 11:1 describes those who "grumble in the face of adversity." How did God respond to their complaints? Are you one who grumbles when things go wrong? When should you rejoice in the Lord?

4. Psalm 106:24–25 outlines four things that the Israelites did. After listing them, write out how each of their actions is either similar or dissimilar to you personally.

5. Ephesians 4:29 tells us to speak good words that edify and give grace to those who hear. List ten things for which you are thankful and talk about these things this week. Try to put on thankful speech rather than complaining and grumbling.

Spend time praying this week that your habits of self-centered, unthankful speech will be replaced by God-honoring speech that will bring glory to Him and encourage others.

Uncommon Service

They are to teach my people the difference between the holy and the common... (Ezekiel 44:23, NIV).

Scripture: 1 Samuel 2:12–17, 33–34; Leviticus 10:1–2;
1 Peter 2:9–10

1. The teachers in the Old Testament were charged to teach people the difference between that which was holy and that which was common. Why would people need to be reminded of this difference?

2. Name some biblical characters (see especially 1 Samuel 2 and Leviticus 10) who viewed their service to God as ordinary or common. What was their fate?

3. How does 1 Peter 2:9–10 describe Christians?

4. If you are a holy nation or a royal priesthood, how should that effect your view of your spiritual duties?

5. What areas of your Christian experience have you begun to view as ordinary or common?

6. What happens to the life-giving power of these things when you don't recognize them as holy or set apart for God?

7. What areas of UV have you begun to view as ordinary or common?

8. What will you do this week to remember your holy commitment to the Lord on this program?

Spend time praying this week that you will walk your Christian life by faith. It's very easy to think, "ho-hum, I've done this a thousand times before. It's no big deal." Remember that it is the Lord Jesus Christ that you are serving.

What Does God See?

And there is no creature hidden from His sight, but all things are open and laid bare to the eyes of Him with whom we have to do (Hebrews 4:13).

Scripture: 1 Samuel 16:7; Psalm 18:28; Jeremiah 17:10

1. After reading 1 Samuel 16:7, do you think that God is primarily concerned about how much you weigh?

2. What does God look at when He measures us?

3. Psalm 18:28 teaches that the Lord "illumines" our darkness. What does this mean generally and specifically as it relates to UV?

4. When you refuse to deal with problem areas in your life, does it mean that God is also ignoring them?

5. What does Jeremiah 17:10 tell us God does?

6. Since we know that God knows everything about us, not only our actions, but also what motivates those actions, what should our response to Him be?

7. List the areas in your life that you have been hiding from God and ask Him now to help you face and deal with them.

Spend time this week meditating on the fact that the Lord sees you as you are, and yet He loves you.

Whom Are You Seeking to Please?

...and circumcision is that which is of the heart, by the Spirit, not by the letter; and his praise is not from men, but from God (Romans 2:29).

Scripture: 1 Samuel 13:8–13, 15:24; Exodus 4; John 12:42–43

1. As you read the story of King Saul in 1 Samuel, what reasons would Saul have given for his disobedience.

2. What seems to be the desire that motivated him?

3. What eventually happened to King Saul?

4. Did he gain the approval of men? Of God?

5. As you read of Moses' call in the desert, what is the primary factor that prevents him from being God's mouthpiece?

6. According to John 12:42–43, what stopped the religious leaders from confessing Christ?

7. As you look at your own life, how important does the "praise of man" seem to you?

8. What happens when you don't receive the praise that you think you deserve?

9. Are you ever tempted to disobey or ignore God's will because it doesn't fit in to your desire to be approved of by man?

Spend time in prayer this week asking God to cause you to desire to please Him more than anything else in your life. Confess the areas where you have disobeyed and ask Him to help you to love Him more than any other thing.

Who Is In Control?

The earth is the LORD'S and all that it contains, the world, and those who dwell in it (Psalm 24:1).

Scripture: Daniel 4:35; Jonah 1:2–3, 4:1–4, 9; Psalm 37:1–11

1. Why did Jonah refuse to go to Nineveh? (Jonah 1:2–3; 4:1–4, 9)

2. What were the emotions that he had in response to not getting his own way? (4:1–4, 9)

3. What blessings did he miss out on because he was consumed with the desire to control the events in his life?

4. As you think about your life, are there any areas in which you refuse to obey the Lord? What are those areas?

5. Do you ever refuse to obey Him because you think that your way is better or you like the illusion of being "in control"?

6. We need to grapple with the reality that the Lord really is in control and that He is working His own plan out in our lives. What does Daniel 4:35 teach about this?

7. After reading Psalm 37:1–11, list the actions and attitudes that we should put off and put on.

Spend time in prayer this week, praying that every part of your life will be committed to Him and that you will give Him complete control of your heart and life.

Who Is Your Savior?

Come to ME, *all who are weary and heavy-laden, and I will give you rest. Take My yoke upon you, and learn from Me, for I am gentle and humble in heart; and* YOU SHALL FIND REST FOR YOUR SOULS (Matthew 11:28–29).

Scripture: Psalm 16:11; Matthew 1:21

1. What does the term "Savior" mean to you?

2. When you feel weary and heavy-laden, where do you normally turn?

3. Where should you turn?

4. Do you find "rest for your soul" when you turn to someone/ something other than Christ? What do you find?

5. After reading Psalm 16:11, what can you expect to find in the presence of the Lord?

6. The name "Jesus" means "Savior." (See Matthew 1:21.) What has Jesus saved you from?

7. List things that you are still awaiting salvation from:

Spend time this week praying that you will see an even greater salvation worked in you. Spend time coming to Jesus and learning of Him. Find rest in Him this week.

Whose Righteousness?

...and may be found in Him, not having a righteousness of my own derived from the *Law, but that which is through faith in Christ...* (Philippians 3:9).

Scripture: Hebrews 13:9; 1 Corinthians 1:30; 2 Corinthians 5:21

1. What does the term "righteousness" mean?

2. Where does 1 Corinthians 1:30 and 2 Corinthians 5:21 say that our righteousness as Christians come from?

3. When you think about your standing before God, on what do you base your confidence?

4. When you think about the problems you have, do you sometimes have the attitude that says, "I can handle this on my own"? Describe a situation where this was true of your attitude.

5. After reading Hebrews 13:9, state what the phrase "strengthened by grace, not by foods" means.

6. Take time now to commit to the Lord areas of your life (especially UV) in which you have been relying on your own strength to produce a "works righteousness before God." List these areas:

Pray this week that you will have a new understanding of grace and the righteousness that is by faith.

Worry and Anxiety

And do not seek what you shall eat, and what you shall drink, and do not keep worrying (Luke 12:29).

Scripture: Matthew 6:31–33; Luke 12:22–24; Luke 21:34;
Philippians 4:6–8; 1 Peter 5:6–7

1. What are the assurances that we receive after reading Matthew 6:31–33 and Luke 12:22–24?

2. What things in your life cause you to worry and subsequently to eat?

3. Luke 21:34 tells us to "be on guard" against worry. What does this mean?

4. Jesus linked worry with an undisciplined life. How do these two things feed into each other?

5. 1 Peter 5:6–7 and Philippians 4:6–8 tell us to do certain things when we are anxious. What are they and how do they relate to your life?

Ask the Lord to help you see the areas in which you are lacking His peace and start today to "cast your cares upon Him." Pray for wisdom to see when you are eating due to anxiety and ask Him to help you trust Him instead.

Zeal – Your Warm Covering

...that He might redeem us from every lawless deed and purify for Himself a people for His own possession, zealous for good deeds. (Titus 2:14)

Scripture: John 2:14–17; Isaiah 59:17; 1 Corinthians 3:9

1. What does the word "zeal" mean?

2. Jesus was one who had great zeal. For what things was He zealous?

3. When you consider God calling you the "building of God," what kind of attitude should you have?

4. How does John 2:14–17 relate to you?

5. Isaiah 59:17 describes zeal in what terms?

6. What is the function of a cloak or mantle?

7. What is God building in your life now?

8. What is your attitude toward His work in you?

9. Is it what it should be?

10. How would enthusiasm toward looking thin and a zeal to see God's purpose in you differ?

11. Which one will sustain and "warm" you?

Spend time this week thinking about the work of God in your life and thanking Him for it. Ask Him to wrap you in a "cloak of zeal" which will protect you from any distractions.

The Fear of The Lord

Charm is deceitful and beauty is vain, but a woman who fears the LORD, she shall be praised (Proverbs 31:30).

Scripture: Proverbs 31:10ff.; 1 Peter 3:3–4, 5:5; Isaiah 61:10; 1 Timothy 2:9–10

1. In what ways are charm deceitful and beauty vain?

2. Have you sought after charm or beauty? Why? To what cultural forces are you acquiescing when you seek to look good to the world?

3. Is it wrong to try to look good? Why or why not? In what ways could trying to "look good" be sinful? Does this mean that we shouldn't be concerned at all about how we look?

4. What does it mean to "fear the Lord?" (Proverbs 31:30)

5. What are the qualities that God finds so precious in a woman listed in 1 Peter 3:3–4? What is a woman who has these qualities like? How interested are you in developing them? Examine the ways that you spend your time in pursuit of inner and outer beauty.

6. Read Isaiah 61:10, 1 Peter 5:5, and 1 Timothy 2:9–10. What is God's attitude toward the pursuit of outward beauty?

Spend time this week praying that you will become a woman who fears the Lord, who is known by her godly qualities.

Changed Into His Image

For whom He foreknew, He also predestined to become conformed to the image of His Son, that He might be the first-born among many brethren... (Romans 8:29).

Scripture: Romans 8:28–29; 1 Samuel 16:7; 1 Thessalonians 3:11–13

1. What is God's goal for your life? (Romans 8:28–29)

2. Is God interested in how much you weigh? Why or why not?

3. In what is God interested? (1 Samuel 16:7) What does this mean?

4. What image does God want you to pursue? (1 Thessalonians 3:11–13)

5. If God doesn't care about our appearance, why should we seek to develop godly eating habits?

6. If we are focused on trying to look good, will we ever have the peace and joy that God desires for us? Why or why not?

Spend time praying that God will help you to have His motives as you learn to eat in a more godly way.

Self-Discipline – The Result of the Spirit's Work

But when the Holy Spirit controls our lives he will produce this kind of fruit in us: love, joy, peace, patience, kindness, goodness, faithfulness, gentleness and self-control... (Galatians 5:22-23, TLB).

Scripture: Philippians 1:11; 2:12–13; John 15:2–5, 16; Romans 7:4; Colossians 1:10

1. Read Galatians 5:22–23. List the fruit or result of the Spirit's work in the Christian's life.

2. What are the implications of the truth that this is the Spirit's work?

3. Can you do anything to change your heart or character? (Philippians 2:12–13)

4. What does it mean to be "self-controlled"?

5. Jesus spoke in depth about fruitfulness in John 15. What are the principles He was teaching? How should these principles impact your life?

6. Read Romans 7:4, Colossians 1:10, and Philippians 1:11. Each verse tells us that God's goal for us is fruitfulness. What else can you learn about becoming fruitful from these passages?

Spend time praying this week that you will be thankful for God's promise to conform your character to His own. This is not something that we would ever desire or accomplish on our own, and yet God has committed Himself to this task. Ask Him to show you ways that you might cooperate with His work.

A Heart Focused on Glorifying God

*So whether you eat or drink or whatever you do, do it all for
the glory of God* (1 Corinthians 10:31, NIV).

1. There are five principles to be considered as you seek to develop
    godly eating habits. Write out your thoughts on each of these
    principles below.

    a. In everything you do (including eating), you should seek to
        glorify God.

    b. God is interested in changing you so that you may reflect
        Christ's image to others.

    c. The pursuit of beauty and thinness is not a God-centered
        goal, per se.

    d. Your body is the temple of God's Spirit.

    e. Self-control or self-discipline is a fruit of the Spirit's work.

Do you have any questions about any of these principles? Write them
out and be prepared to discuss them in class next week.

2. Write out the D-I-S-C-I-P-L-I-N-E-D Eating Questions below (I've done the first one for you). Begin today to ask God for help in memorizing these questions and verses (see pp. 16, 87).

D oubt – Do I *doubt* that I can eat this food without sinning? (Romans 14:23)

I

S

C

I

P

L

I

N

E

D

E (ating)

How do you think that reviewing these questions will impact your eating habits?

Spend time praying that God will enlighten, encourage, and strengthen you this week as you seek to develop new, godly eating habits.

Doubt

But he who doubts is condemned if he eats, because his eating is *not from faith; and whatever is not from faith is sin* (Romans 14:23).

Scripture: 1 Corinthians 6:12; 10:23; Acts 15:20; Romans 14:17

1. Write out the first principle "D" in the "Disciplined Eating" acrostic.

2. What controversy was Paul speaking of in Romans 14?

3. Since most of us are not concerned about eating food offered to idols, how would this passage relate to us today?

4. Can you think of any foods that the Bible specifically tells you not to eat? If so, what are they? What did Paul mean when he said, "All things are lawful for me?" (1 Corinthians 6:12 and 10:23)

5. The council in Jerusalem discussed dietary restrictions and issued directions to Christians (Acts 15:20). How do their new guidelines affect believers today?

6. Christians have great liberty to eat and drink (Romans 14:17), but must not violate their consciences. Are there any specific foods that you cannot "eat in faith"?

7. Even though you might have Christian liberty to eat and drink according to your desires, why should you abstain from certain foods?

Spend time this week praying that God would strengthen your conscience so that you can enjoy your liberty in Christ, and also that you would be careful not to violate your conscience by eating anything that you can't eat in faith.

Idolatry: Who Is Your God?

"You shall have no other gods before Me... You shall not worship them or serve them..." (Exodus 20:3, 5a).

Scripture: Philippians 3:19; Matthew 22:36–40; Deuteronomy 6:5

1. Define the word "idol."

2. Are there any idols in your life? (Remember: You can define an idol as anything that takes the place of God in your heart – anything that you love, worship, or serve more than the Lord. You can pinpoint an idol by looking at your habitual sins. It's usually in these areas that you are serving a different god.)

3. In Philippians 3:19, Paul refers to people whose "appetite" was their god. What is the meaning of the word "appetite"?

4. How does it relate to you in this program?

5. When you feel spiritual or emotional emptiness, what should you do?

6. How can you replace the idols in your heart with God? (Matthew 22:36–38; Deuteronomy 6:4)

7. What would the sole worship of the Living God mean in your life, specifically as you have committed to UV?

Spend time praying this week that you will learn what it means to fully love the Lord and to have no other gods in your life.

Stumbling – Loving Others
As You Love Yourself

It is not good to eat meat or to drink wine, or to do anything by which your brother stumbles (Romans 14:21).

Scripture: Matthew 22:37–40; 1 Corinthians 8:8–13; Romans 14:13; Romans 15:1–2

1. Read Matthew 22:37–40. What are the two commands and one implied assumption in these verses?

2. What would it mean to "love others as you love yourself" in the context of UV?

3. Read the passages in 1 Corinthians 8:8–13 and Romans 14:13. What are the principles that Paul is teaching about personal liberty and the law of love?

4. How should these principles about eating food offered to idols effect you when dealing with other, weaker Christians?

5. Write out Romans 15:1–2 below. What is the principle you are to follow when making choices about your liberty.

6. We are to guard carefully our liberty in Christ and not allow ourselves to be in bondage to any man-made laws. In addition, we are not to bind another's conscience by forcing man-made laws on him. In the light of these truths, however, what must our attitude be towards those whose consciences are either weaker (believing that it is sinful for them to do something God has not forbidden) or stronger (those who are able to, in faith, do things that would stumble you)?

Spend time praying this week that God would help you to love others more that you love yourself or your liberty in Christ.

Coveting – "It Just Looks So Good"

"You shall not covet...anything that belongs to your neighbor..." (Exodus 20:17).

Scripture: Genesis 3:1–6; Acts 20:33; Luke 12:15;
1 Corinthians 6:9–11

1. Read Genesis 3:1–6. What were the steps to sin that Eve took?

2. What does the word "covet" mean? In the New Testament, it is synonymous with what other words?

3. Paul's testimony in Acts 20:33 is astounding. What is it? Could you make a statement like that?

4. How do television commercials function to stir up covetousness or greed in your life? Can you think of a specific time when this happened?

5. Jesus warns us about coveting or greed in Luke 12:15. What is the truth that He teaches in this verse? How would that truth help you in this program?

6. In 1 Corinthians 6:9–10 we find a list of sins that are committed by unbelievers. What does verse 11 teach? How does this encourage you?

Spend time in prayer this week that God would enable you to see the things you frequently covet and that He would help you to desire or covet Him alone.

Inroad – A Door to More Sin

Put on the Lord Jesus Christ, and make no provision for the flesh in regard to its *lusts* (Romans 13:14).

Scripture: Colossians 3:10–12; Romans 6:16, 8:12–13; Galatians 5:24

1. What does Paul mean in Colossians 3:10–12 when he says, "...put on the new self"?

2. Specifically, how could you do this in your life?

3. In Romans 8:12–13 Paul states that we are not "under obligation" to the flesh. What does this mean? Do you live as though you owed your old nature obedience?

4. In Galatians 5:24 Paul teaches that those who belong to Christ have crucified their flesh and its lusts. How would you explain this concept to a young believer?

5. In reference to your eating habits, are their lusts that you still need to crucify? What are they?

6. How does giving in to these desires create a habitual inroad for more sin in your life (Romans 6:16)?

Spend time in prayer this week, praying that you would see the areas in your life where you "make provision for your flesh," particularly through your eating. Plead with God to give you a heart that would hate sin and not desire to coddle it.

Praise – Developing A Thankful Heart

*For everything created by God is good, and nothing is to be
rejected, if it is received with gratitude; for it is sanctified by
means of the word of God and prayer* (1 Timothy 4:4-5).

Scripture: Psalm 9:1–2, 111:1–2; Colossians 2:6–7; Philippians 4:8

1. In Psalm 9:1–2, how does David give thanks?

2. Relate some of the wonders God has performed in your life.

3. Psalm 111:1–2 give instructions about where to give thanks and what things to be thankful for. What are they?

4. According to Colossians 2:6–7, what are the instructions to those who have received Christ Jesus the Lord?

5. What do you think "overflowing with gratitude" means?

6. What are the items listed in Philippians 4:8 that we should think about?

If we spend time thinking "on these things" – the wonderful things that God has done in our lives – our hearts truly will overflow with gratitude. Take time this week to give thanks for God's grace in your life. You can do it in song, in testimony to others, or in a life filled with joy.

Life – Your Body, God's Home

Or do you not know that your body is a temple of the Holy Spirit who is in you, whom you have from God, and that you are not your own? For you have been bought with a price; therefore glorify God in your body (1 Corinthians 6:19-20).

Scripture: 1 Corinthians 3:16, 6:19–20; Ephesians 2:21–22; 1 Peter 2:5; Exodus 20:13

1. What does the phrase "your body is a temple of the Holy Spirit" (1 Corinthians 3:16, 6:19–20) mean?

2. Why is it important for you to think about your body in these terms?

3. Are you presently experiencing any physical problems caused by ungodly eating habits? If so, what?

4. What steps can you take to overcome these problems? God is gracious and can heal and restore your life as you seek to glorify Him in your body.

5. God calls you his "building," and "living stones" (Ephesians 2:21–22; 1 Peter 2:5). What does this mean about your obligation to seek to be healthy?

6. What does the Sixth Commandment teach (Exodus 20:13)? How should this teaching impact your eating habits?

Spend time in prayer this week, praying that God would help you to view your body as His temple and that you would take the time to care for your health to honor and glorify Him.

Illustration – Your Life, A Living Epistle

...show yourself an example of those who believe
(1 Timothy 4:12b).

Scripture: 2 Corinthians 3:2; 1 Corinthians 11:1;
1 Thessalonians 2:10–12; Titus 2:7–8

1. Paul said that the Corinthians were an epistle, "known and read of all men" (2 Corinthians 3:2, KJV). What did he mean?

2. Who are the people in your life that are reading you?

3. What would they say about your love for God, for others, and for food?

4. Paul could say that he wanted others to imitate him. Although we might not be so bold as to say that, we must realize that others (especially our children) will imitate us. Can you think of people that you imitate or that imitate you? In light of this principle, how important is your example? (1 Corinthians 11:1, 1 Thessalonians 2:10–12).

5. What are the qualities that Paul lists in Titus 2:7–8 that we should seek to model for others? Which ones of these do you think you do well with? Which ones need work?

Ask members of your family (or others that you are with regularly) to help you see what attitudes and behaviors you are modeling (especially with your eating habits). What kind of influence are you on your friends? Pray that God would use your life as His means to draw others to Himself and to help others see that they can have hope and trust in God.

Just Say "No"

...I buffet my body and make it my slave, lest possibly, after I have preached to others, I myself should be disqualified (1 Corinthians 9:27).

Scripture: 1 Corinthians 6:12–13; 9:25; 4:11–12;
2 Corinthians 6:4–5; 11:27; 1 Peter 2:11

1. Although Paul rejoiced in his liberty (1 Corinthians 6:12–13), he balanced his liberty with what principle?

2. Do you ask yourself if your actions, although you may have liberty in them, are profitable? Are you enslaved by them in any way?

3. Paul uses the allegory of the athlete in 1 Corinthians 9:25. What principle is he striving to teach when he says that these athletes compete for perishable prizes, while we for imperishable?

4. Are you consciously aware of the self-discipline that you must exercise to win in your walk with the Lord?

5. Paul describes his life in 1 Corinthians 4:11–12, 2 Corinthians 6:4–5 and 11:27. What was he willing to suffer for Christ? Do you think that he would have been able to go through these trials if he wasn't disciplined, especially when it came to his daily life?

6. Do you see yourself as a person who has to have certain foods or comforts? Are you willing to suffer for the kingdom's sake?

7. Do you ever fast for the Lord's sake?

8. Peter encourages us to put to death those desires of our flesh that wage war against our soul (1 Peter 2:11). How do our desires "wage war," and how can we put them to death?

Unless you struggle with anorectic behaviors, choose at least one meal this week to which you're going to say "no" and spend the time in prayer. Ask God to show you any foods or comforts that you feel you must have and offer them up as a sacrifice for a time, for Him.

Emotional Eating

"If you do well, will not your countenance be lifted up? And if you do not do well, sin is crouching at the door; and its desire is for you, but you must master it" (Genesis 4:7).

Scripture: Acts 10:34–35; Romans 2:7, 14:16–18

1. Write out the first "E" D-I-S-C-I-P-L-I-N-E-D Eating question.

2. Are emotions themselves sinful? Why or why not?

3. Where do emotions come from?

4. The Lord advised Cain that "doing well" would change his emotional state. How should this advice change your response to your emotions?

5. How can you master the "sin that is crouching at the door"?

6. Do you ever eat because of your emotional state? Describe this pattern.

7. When you are depressed, fearful, or angry, how should you respond?

8. Read Acts 10:34–35 and Romans 2:7 and 14:16–18. We can know that we are accepted by God and have our "countenance lifted up" when we act in certain ways. What are they?

Spend time in prayer this week that you will use your emotions for God's glory and learn to do what is right, no matter how you feel. As you practice this lifestyle, you'll soon find your emotions following along.

What's Distracting You?

But the Lord answered and said to her, "Martha, Martha, you are worried and bothered about so many things; but only a few things are necessary, really only one, for Mary has chosen the good part, which shall not be taken away from her" (Luke 10:41–42).

Scripture: Mark 4:19; Luke 21:34; Matthew 6:25–34;
Psalm 73:25; 142:5

1. Martha was worried and bothered about her meal preparations and missed the reality that the Son of God was sitting in her living room. In what ways are you like her?

2. Mark 4:19 and Luke 21:34 teach that worries and distractions will cause you to be unfruitful in your walk with Christ. What are the worries and distractions that draw your heart away?

3. Reflect now especially in the area of your cooking or preparing to have guests for dinner. Are you more like Martha or Mary? Do you ever consider spending less time preparing a meal and more time preparing your heart to minister to your guests? How could you do better at this?

4. Jesus outlines the process of worry in Matthew 6:25–34. What can you learn from this passage about the foolishness and true nature of worry?

5. Can you say with the Psalmist that you desire only Him and that you rejoice because He is your portion? What are you desiring when you worry and allow yourself to become distracted from the "good part" that Mary found?

Ask some friends over for dinner. Serve good but plain food and make it a point to minister to them in some way. Ask the Lord to help you to be more concerned about "giving a cup of cold water" to the Lord (with your guests) than impressing them with your housekeeping skills.

Enslaved – Your Freedom in Christ

All things are lawful for me, but not all things are profitable. All things are lawful for me but I will not be mastered by anything (1 Corinthians 6:12).

Scripture: Romans 6:6–7, 16–18; 2 Peter 2:19b; 1 John 3:8b;
2 Corinthians 5:17; 1 Peter 5:6–10

1. In Romans 6:16–18, what does Paul teach regarding your slavery to sin?

2. After reading 2 Peter 2:19b identify areas where you may become enslaved to sin. What does being "overcome" by sin mean?

3. What is one reason why Jesus appeared? (See 1 John 3:8)

4. How does Christ's victory over Satan impact your life?

5. What is God's answer to your old, sinful nature? (Romans 6:6–7)

6. Are there any ways that you are resurrecting your old nature?

7. What does 2 Corinthians 5:17 mean to you personally?

8. What are the four steps to progressive liberty in 1 Peter 5:6–10?

Spend time in prayer this week that God will make your freedom a very precious, vital truth in your life. Pray that He will reveal areas where you are in bondage and will make you wholly desire to follow Him in everything.

D-I-S-C-I-P-L-I-N-E-D E-ating Questions

Doubt — Do I *doubt* that I can eat this food without sinning?

But he who doubts is condemned if he eats, because his eating is not from faith; and whatever is not from faith is sin (Romans 14:23).

Idolatry — Will eating this food demonstrate a heart of idolatry?

"You shall have no other gods before Me" (Exodus 20:3).

Stumble — Will eating this cause a weaker Christian to stumble?

It is good not to eat meat or to drink wine, or to do anything by which your brother stumbles (Romans 14:21).

Coveting — Am I eating this food because I am coveting it?

"You shall not covet your neighbor's house; you shall not covet your neighbor's wife or his male servant or his female servant or his ox or his donkey or anything that belongs to your neighbor" (Exodus 20:17).

Inroad — If I eat this food will it create an inroad for sin in my life?

But put on the Lord Jesus Christ, and make no provision for the flesh in regard to its lusts (Romans 13:14).

Praise — Can I eat this food with praise and gratitude?

For everything created by God is good, and nothing is to be rejected, if it is received with gratitude (1 Timothy 4:4).

Life — Would eating this food harm my life or health in any way?

"You shall not murder" (Exodus 20:13)

Illustrate — Am I illustrating good eating habits for others?

Let no one look down on your youthfulness, but rather in speech, conduct, love, faith and purity, show yourself an example of those who believe (1 Timothy 4:12).

No — Am I able to just say "No"?

…but I buffet my body and make it my slave, lest possibly, after I have preached to others, I myself should be disqualified (1 Corinthians 9:27).

Emotions — Does my desire to eat this flow out of any sinful emotions?

> "If you do well, will not your countenance be lifted up: And if you do not do well, sin is crouching at the door; and its desire is for you, but you must master it" (Genesis 4:7).

Distract — Will eating or preparing this food distract me from something better?

> But the Lord answered and said to her, "Martha, Martha, you are worried and bothered about so many things; but only a few things are necessary, really only one, for Mary has chosen the good part, which shall not be taken away from her" (Luke 10:41–42).

Enslave — Will eating this food enslave me in any way?

> All things are lawful for me, but not all things are profitable. All things are lawful for me, but I will not be mastered by anything (1 Corinthians 6:12).

Daily
Diary

MONDAY	D	TUESDAY	D	WEDNESDAY	D
Meats		Meats		Meats	
Grains		Grains		Grains	
Fruits		Fruits		Fruits	
Vegetables		Vegetables		Vegetables	
Dairy		Dairy		Dairy	
Other		Other		Other	
WATER ❑ ❑ ❑		WATER ❑ ❑ ❑		WATER ❑ ❑ ❑	
Cal/Fat Total		Cal/Fat Total		Cal/Fat Total	
Prayer Time Bible Chpts. Exercise		Prayer Time Bible Chpts. Exercise		Prayer Time Bible Chpts. Exercise	
Victories Needed Growth		Victories Needed Growth		Victories Needed Growth	

THURSDAY	D	FRIDAY	D	SATURDAY	D	SUNDAY	D
Meats		Meats		Meats		Meats	
Grains		Grains		Grains		Grains	
Fruits		Fruits		Fruits		Fruits	
Vegetables		Vegetables		Vegetables		Vegetables	
Dairy		Dairy		Dairy		Dairy	
Other		Other		Other		Other	
WATER ❐ ❐ ❐		WATER ❐ ❐ ❐		WATER ❐ ❐ ❐		WATER ❐ ❐ ❐	
Cal/Fat Total		Cal/Fat Total		Cal/Fat Total		Cal/Fat Total	
Prayer Time		Prayer Time		Prayer Time		Prayer Time	
Bible Chpts.		Bible Chpts.		Bible Chpts.		Bible Chpts.	
Exercise		Exercise		Exercise		Exercise	
Victories		Victories		Victories		Victories	
Needed Growth		Needed Growth		Needed Growth		Needed Growth	

	Monday	D		Tuesday	D		Wednesday	D
	Meats 4 oz hamburger	I		Meats 2 eggs 1/2 c tuna			Meats 2 hot dogs 3 sl turkey	L
	Grains 2 sl toast 1/2 c noodles corn chips	E		Grains English muffin 2 sl bread 2 c pasta			Grains HD bun 2 sl bread popcorn	N
	Fruits orange 12 grapes			Fruits no fruit	L		Fruits apple peach	
	Vegetables salad w/ tomatoes & nonfat dressing			Vegetables salad w/pasta fresh tomato sauce			Vegetables corn on the cob salad w/nf dressing	
	Dairy NF milk			Dairy yogurt			Dairy none	
	Other 2 T mayo	E		Other 1 T mayo			Other mayo butter on popcorn	
	WATER ☑ ☑ ☐			WATER ☑ ☐ ☐			WATER ☑ ☑ ☐	
	Cal/Fat Total			Cal/Fat Total			Cal/Fat Total	
	Prayer Time 7:30 am Bible Chpts. John 1–2 Exercise walked 1 mile			Prayer Time 7:30 am Bible Chpts. John 3–4 Exercise none			Prayer Time 8:00 am Bible Chpts. -0- Exercise walked 1 mile	
	Victories walked! Needed Growth angry – ate chips			Victories read & prayed 2 days Needed Growth exercise			Victories read Needed Growth woke up late, didn't read, overate	

Thursday	D	Friday	D	Saturday	D	Sunday	D
Meats 2 sl ham 4 oz steak	N	Meats 3 oz cheese 4 oz halibut		Meats 2 eggs 2 hot dogs 6 oz hamburger	C	Meats meatballs chicken breast	
Grains 2 sl bread 5 oz potato		Grains 4 sl bread 1 cup rice		Grains 4 pancakes 2 HD buns 1 HD bun	C	Grains 1 c pasta 1/2 c br. rice popcorn	
Fruits pear orange juice		Fruits grapefruit apple		Fruits none		Fruits fruit salad	
Vegetables 1 c gr. beans salad w/nf dressing		Vegetables salad w/nf dressing peas		Vegetables none		Vegetables salad w/nf dressing fresh gr. beans	
Dairy ice cream	N	Dairy yogurt		Dairy IC	C	Dairy yogurt	
Other too much sour cream	N	Other marg. on rice		Other toppings on IC/mayo	C	Other butter on popcorn	
WATER ☑ ☑ ☑		WATER ☑ ☑ ☐		WATER ☑ ☑ ☑		WATER ☐ ☐ ☐	
Cal/Fat Total		Cal/Fat Total		Cal/Fat Total		Cal/Fat Total	
Prayer Time 7:30 am Bible Chpts. John 5–6 Exercise walked 1 mile		Prayer Time 7:30 am Bible Chpts. John 7–8 Exercise walked 2 miles!		Prayer Time 8:00 am Bible Chpts. -0- Exercise -0-		Prayer Time -0- Bible Chpts. John 9–10 Exercise walked 1 mile	
Victories read & prayed again Needed Growth should've said no to sour cr & steak		Victories Praise God! Great Day! Needed Growth		Victories Needed Growth went to ball game & ignored program!		Victories one week complete Needed Growth consistent prayer	

Daily Diary

93

A Leader's Manual for *Uncommon Vessels* is also available from TIMELESS TEXTS (1-800-814-1045). It includes expanded Bible studies with brief answers, and information and forms to use in setting up an Uncommon Vessels group, in addition to the full content of this basic member's book.